Be Ye PERFECT.

As Your FATHER is PERFECT.

WORKBOOK PRESS LLC
187 E Warm Springs Rd,
Suite B285 Las Vegas NV 89119 USA

Website: https://workbookpress.com/
Hotline: 1-888-818-4856
Email: admin@workbookpress.com

Ordering Information:

Quantity sales. Special discounts are available on quantity purchases by corporations, associations, and others. For details, contact the publisher at the address above.

Library of Congress Control Number:

ISBN-13:   978-1-963718-43-0   Paperback Version
            978-1-963718-44-7   Digital Version

REV. DATE: 02/13/2024

Other Books by The Author

GGG The Grief ,The Grace, & The Glory
(Trilogy) Xlibris

888 Out Spring of 2024 PageTurner Press
and Media..Chula Vista, California

Avoid These Sins..
To Transition Safely Into
the Afterlife..

Table of Contents

Abandonment

Abortion

Abuse

Adultery

Avarice

Arrogance

Argumentative

Bickering

Bribery

Bitterness

Blame shifting

Blasphemy

(Of The Holy Spirit Unforgivable
ithis Life ..and the Life Herafter)

Boastfulness

Brutality

Covetousness

Corruption

Contempt

Conniving

Callousness

Cowardly

Complaining

Chaos

Destruction

Doubt

Dark

Dreadful

Dishonor

Disrespect

Discord

Disbelief

Detestable

Duality

Drunkenness

Envy

Extortion

Exaltation

Fear

False testimony

Forgery

Fornication

Fraud

Gaslighting

Greed

Gossip

Gluttony

Heresy

Heady

Haughty

Hatred

Hypocrisy

Idolatry

Incest

Impurity

Inhumane

Inequality

Lust

Lewdness

Lawlessness

Liars

Laziness

Malice

Manipulation

Mockery

Murder

Narcissism

Nastiness

Nymphomaniac

Occult

Orgies

Opportunist

Opulence

Ouija
(Forbidden)

Pride

Prejudice

Projection

Pornography

Paraphernalia

Perversion

Pedophilia

Psychics

Psychopath

Philandering

Prostitution

Rebellion

Revelry

Sensuality

Sadism

Seance (Forbidden)

Sociopath

Sloth

Slander

Sins of Omission

Spiritual Sloth

Scoffers

Sorcerers

Sodomy

Self-condemned

Suicide

Theft

Unbelief

Unrighteous

Unholy

Unclean

Vanity

Violence

Viciousness

Vengeance

Witchcraft

Warlocks

Wrath

Whoremongers

Worry

Wickedness

Willful Sin

Truth, Faith, Love, Courage, Liberty, Generosity, Charity, Justice, Mercy, Humility

www.ingramcontent.com/pod-product-compliance
Lightning Source LLC
Chambersburg PA
CBHW020918140626
46545CB00015B/302